EARLY INDIAN CULTURE

EARLY INDIAN CULTURE

BY

BIMALA CHURN LAW,

M.A., B.L., PH.D., D.LITT., HON., D. LITT.

(Allahabad University) Hony. Member, Royal Asiatic Society of Great Britain & Ireland; Ex-President, Royal Asiatic Society of Bengal; Fellow, Calcutta University, etc. etc.

GYAN

Published by

Gyan Publishing House
5, Ansari Road
Daryaganj, New Delhi-110002
Phone: 011-47034999, 9811692060
E-mail: books@gyanbooks.com

Distribution Network
gyanbooks.com
India, USA, Canada, UK, Australia, France

ISBN : 978-81-212-2436-9 (HB)
First Published, 1948

2nd Impression 2021

Printed at: Gyan Press, Delhi.

Early Indian Culture
Author: Bimala Churn Law

EARLY INDIAN CULTURE

By

BIMALA CHURN LAW,

M.A., B.L., Ph.D., D.Litt., Hon. D.Litt. (*Allahabad University*)
Hony. Member, Royal Asiatic Society of Great Britain & Ireland;
Ex-President, Royal Asiatic Society of Bengal;
Fellow, Calcutta University, etc., etc.

Published by

THE INDIAN RESEARCH INSTITUTE,
170 MANIKTALA STREET, CALCUTTA.
1948

PREFACE

In my little treatise on *Early Indian Culture* I have traced its history from the earliest times down to the Muslim conquest of India. This treatise is divided into nine sections dealing with Prehistoric, Vedic, Brahmanic, Pre-Maurya, Maurya and Śuṅga, Scythian, Gupta, Later Mediaeval, Āndhra and Dravidian culture. It is a semi-popular treatment which gives a connected account of early Indian culture under different periods of its history. Almost all the original sources and the relevant data from modern literature have been utilised in order to make it interesting. Hope it will be of some use to those for whom it is intended.

Calcutta,
43 Kailas Bose Street,
The 1st March 1948.

B. C. Law.

CONTENTS

BIBLIOGRAPHY

Ancient History of the Deccan (Dubreuil).
Ancient Indian Historical Tradition (F. E. Pargiter)
Ancient Khotan (Stein).
Annals of the Bhandarkar Oriental Research Institute, Vol I, Pt I, 1919
Arthaśāstra of Kautilya (ed by Shamashastri).
Asoka (B. M Barua)
Asoka (D. R Bhandarkar).

Buddhist India (T W. Rhys Davids).
Buddhist Records of the Western World (S Beal)

Cambridge History of India, Vol. I—Ancient India
Candragupta Maurya and His Times (R. K. Mookerjee).
Carmichael Lectures, 1918 (D R. Bhandarkar).
Catalogue of Coins of the Āndhra Dynasty (Rapson).
Chronology of the Late Imperial Guptas (R. D. Banerjee).

Dynasties of the Kali Age (F. E. Pargiter).

Early History of India, 4th ed. (V. A. Smith)
Early History of the Dekhan (R. G. Bhandarkar).
Epigraphia Indica, Vol. V—Keilhorn's List of Northern Inscriptions.

Fā-Hien (Legge).

Gupta Inscriptions (Fleet)

Harṣa (R K. Mookerjee)
History of Fine Art in India and Ceylon (V. A. Smith).

India as described in early texts of Buddhism and Jainism (B. C Law).
Indus Valley Civilisation (Sir John Marshall)
Inscriptions of Aśoka (Sir Alexander Cunningham).

Journal of the Royal Asiatic Society, 1897 and 1911 (Hultzsch).

Mahāvīra: His Life and Teachings (B. C. Law).

Pallava Antiquities, Vol. I—Dravidian Architecture, 1918 (Dubreuil).
Peep into the Early History of India from the foundation of the Maurya dynasty to the downfall of the Imperial Gupta Dynasty, 322 B.C.—*cir.* A.D. 500, A (R. G. Bhandarkar), Bombay, 1900.
Political History of Ancient India, 4th ed. (H. C. Raychaudhuri).

Tamils Eighteen Hundred Years Ago, The (V. K. Pillai).
Théâtre Indien (Sylvain Lévi).

Vedic Index (Macdonell & Keith).
Vedic India (Ragozin).

Watters On Yuan Chwang's Travels in India.

Section I

PREHISTORIC

Pre-Chellean may be taken as the best term to denote the earliest stage of culture in which men lived with animals. The celt, the only kind of rude stone implement, was the first handicraft of the Palæolithic men in India and Burma. The Narmada celt is of pointed oval shape. The Godāvarī 'agate-chip' seems to indicate a slight advance in craftsmanship from the Narmada celt. All such implements were used as the hunting weapons in the remote age when men struggled very hard for existence. The early and middle Palæolithic Indian settlements are found in the Districts of Cuddapah, Guntur and Nellore and the neighbourhood of Madras. It is no wonder that Cuddapah was found most attractive for the primitive settlers. More than 200 specimens of 'old Artefacts' have been discovered here. The settlements of Indian Acheullean and Mousterian are found along the Attrampakkam stream of the Chingleput district. Early palæolithic cave-dwellers were mighty hunters and they acquired the knowledge of lighting fire and keeping it ablaze. Palæolithic men were rude savages who had no idea of building houses or huts. Agriculture was quite unknown to them. They clothed themselves with skins or grass-mats. Social and economic activities hardly developed among these peoples. The Neoliths largely settled in the Salem, Madura and Bellary districts. Like the Palæoliths, they were more vegetarians than carnivorous. Colour had more fascination for them. They lived mostly on the hills and in the shallow sloping valleys. They honoured the departed souls with tombs built of massive stones. Much is not known of the civilisation of the Bronze age. The articles belonging to this age consist of costly ornaments rather than articles of daily use. The Copper age antiquities have been obtained from Rajpur, Mathura, Mainpuri, Niarai, Bithur, Allahabad, Bihar, Hazaribagh, Karachi and Baluchistan. Most of the copperfinds are heavy weapons. The Indian peoples of the Iron age seem to have made the Palni hills as their favourite haunt. They were agriculturists. They wore clothes and knew the art of weaving. They used gold and also bronze as personal ornaments and were specially fond of gold diadems for the head. They used elephants for riding. They were fond of wire bangles, ear-ornaments, bronze diadems and necklaces of stone. The women were fond of dressing their hair elaborately. The excavation of the ancient sites at Harappa and Mohenjodaro in the Punjab and Sind respectively has brought to light many archæological finds, proving the existence of a grand Chalcolithic civilisation in the Indus valleys, upper and lower. At Mohenjodaro and Harappa we have densely populated cities with solid commodious houses of brick, equipped with adequate sanitation, bathrooms, wells and other amenities. Among the Indus people silver is commoner than gold. Utensils and vessels are sometimes made of stone. They have the bow and arrow, spear, dagger, axe and mace. Defensive armour is quite unknown to them. Fish is a common article of diet and so are the turtles and other aquatic creatures. The horse seems to have been unknown to them. It may on the whole be regarded as Pre-horse age. The cow is of no account. Tiger and elephant are familiar to them. Iconism is apparent everywhere in Mohenjodaro and Harappa. The buildings at Mohenjodaro show no decoration. Crude brick was used only for foundations or for the packing of terraces. The walls above the ground were built of burnt bricks, laid in mud or in mud and gypsum mortar combined. They had their foundations, floors, doorways, and windows, lintels and arches, stairways, wells, fire-places, bathrooms, drains, roofs, etc., giving clear evidence to the development of the art of town-planning.

The Indus people cultivated wheat and barley. Their food comprised dates, cereals, beef, mutton, pork and poultry, turtles and tortoises, dried fish, etc. Their dietary must have included milk, vegetables and fruits.

They were not only familiar with gold and silver but also with copper, tin and lead. Besides bronze an alloy of copper and arsenic was in use. Semi-precious stones, e.g., rock-crystal, jasper, blood-stone, plasma, etc., were used for beads and other ornaments. Bitumen was used for waterproofing. Vitrified paste played an important part in the industrial life. Spinning was practised in the houses of the rich and the poor. Most of the Indus pottery was wheelmade, well fired and plain. Spindlewhorls, fresh rubber, cake-moulds and toys were earthenware domestic articles.

As regards the dress of the people, a male figure is seen wearing a long shawl drawn over the left shoulder, and under the right, leaving the right arm free. Men wore short beards and whiskers.

The Indus people had for their games marble and dice. Writing appears as an art which is in extensive use. The script invented by the Indus people for their writing belongs to the same order as the Sumerian, Minian or Egyptian.

As for the disposal of the dead, cremation seems to have been the usual method. It seems likely that the remnants of calcined bones were either ground to powder and cast into the river or disposed of in some other way. The examples of complete burial are rare as also the practice of exposing the dead to wild animals and then burying the remnants, if any, of the excarnated bones.

The Phallic worship of Yonis, male and female, played ostensibly an important part in the religious life of the people. The practice of *Yoga* appears to have played a significant rôle and it was associated with the primitive form of *Śiva*. Tree spirits too seem to have their due place in popular cults.

SECTION II

VEDIC

Vedic civilisation came to replace a matriarchal by a patriarchal form of society. Father is the head of the family and enjoys as such considerable power and absolute right over all other members of his household. Father is the idol of family life. He is the pivot of household organisation, lording over his wife and children. Wife has a large share in the management of the household. She is the mistress of the family, a partner in her husband's religious duties and social obligations, keeping the sacred household fire, and offering oblations unto it, from day to day. Without offspring there can be no paternal tie. In the event of there being no such offspring, the father might have had recourse to adoption but this practice is disapproved in a Ṛgvedic hymn.

Marriage is highly valued as an institution for the maintenance of the family organisation and preservation of society. The marriage ceremony consists in the solemn acceptance of each other by the bride and bridegroom and the bringing of the bride from her father's house to that of her husband. Women in Ṛgvedic society show themselves freely before the public in popular feasts, dances and on similar occasions. There might be stray cases of unprotected women who gave themselves up to prostitution.

Each family consisted of a group of individuals. Branches of one and the same family probably settled in adjoining areas. The cluster of such people or the assemblage of several individual families around a particular area gave rise to a village or *grāma* whose leader was called *grāmaṇi*. Such villages or family units combined together to form a canton of which the leader was called *Viśpati*.

The Vedic Aryans seem to have lived in villages. The idea of society based upon division of labour did not fully develop itself. The Ṛgveda mentions four castes, priest (*Brāhmaṇa*), prince or warrior (*Rājanya*), the commoner (*Vaiśya*) and *Śūdra*. We do not find any mention of a hereditary caste system, comprising within it the lower order of farmers, cattle-traders, labourers, artisans and merchants. But the division of people into four castes based apparently on an organic conception of society was rather Brahmanical than Vedic.

In the Ṛgvedic and even in later Vedic ages, we find instances in which the head of the family performs sacrifices and ceremonies for himself with his wife without any priestly aid. The growth of complication in society naturally tends to the division of labour. The Ṛgveda refers to the acquisition and gift of slaves.

The Vedic Indian stands before us perfectly well-dressed, caring for dress and creating an art of making dress. The garments are found to be both coloured and uncoloured. Two or three garments seem to have formed the usual dress of the people. The cotton and woollen garments were in use; the skins of animals too were used as a clothing; and the rich dress was inlaid with gold. The Ṛgveda speaks of splendid garments, dyed garments, embroidered garments, bridal garments, etc. Ornaments were generally made of gold and included necklaces, ear-rings, anklets and bracelets. Dressing of hair was a common custom among men and women. Shaving though not unknown was not commonly done in the matter of beards.

The Vedic Indians appear to have lived mainly on vegetables and fruits. Milk and clarified butter were used as food. The flesh of goats, sheep, or oxen was eaten by them. The Vedic Aryans though a nation of meat-eaters appear to have had a general aversion to fish, as there is no mention of fishing in the Vedas.

The juice of the somaplant served as a favourite sacrificial drink. Three meals a day were usually taken, once in the morning, once at mid-day, and the third in the evening.

Hospitality went hand in hand with bounty and was regarded as a social virtue as well as a necessity.

The chariot race was a favourite diversion of the people. The game of dice seems to have attracted gamblers. People were fond of singing and dancing. The practice of taming and guarding the tamed elephant was in vogue.

In the Vedic sacrifices, the libation consisted of fresh barley, parched grains, curds, butter and cakes. The dishes comprised varieties of cooked food, gruel, and porridge, fried or parched grains of rice and fruits.

The three different methods of the disposal of the dead consisted of burial, exposure and cremation.

Cattle-rearing seems to have been the chief occupation of the Vedic Aryans whose wealth consisted in the maintenance of cows and other useful animals. Cows and bullocks are often praised as the most precious possessions. The milk of the cow was one of the chief articles of food. Horses, asses, goats, sheep, dogs, camels, and buffaloes were known.

to the Vedic Aryans. In the lives of the Vedic Aryans the horse plays an important part. It is suggested that the appearance of horse as domesticated animal was synchronous with the advent of the Bharata princes from Uttarakuru.

The picture of the Indo-Aryan society as portrayed in the Vedas is that of a partly pastoral, partly agricultural people who have not yet emerged from the village state, who have no knowledge of life in cities or of the complex economic organisation which such life implies and whose houses are constructed largely of bamboo.

Hunting seems to have been an usual practice. Pearl fishery existed in the Ṛgvedic period.

There was the hunting of boars with dogs, catching of lions by snares and capture of antelopes in pits.

Agriculture was an occupation of the people. The bull was used in drawing ploughs. Channels were dug for irrigation. During the early Vedic period there was hardly any cultivation save that of wheat and barley.

There were different kinds of industry in the Ṛgvedic period. The tanner used the skin of the oxen and worked it up into strings of bows, leather-bottles and straps. Wood-worker, carriage-builder, and cabinet-maker were in existence. There were smiths or metal-workers. Sewing and weaving of cloth and making of mats from grass or reeds were usually the arts practised by women. The art of spinning and weaving sufficiently developed as handicrafts. The art of washing also developed. In the same family the members were known to have followed different callings.

In the matter of trade, the system of barter was usually resorted to. The Ṛgveda mentions two divisions of the army of the Maruts, viz., the Gaṇas and the Vrātas, both meaning guilds or corporations and incidentally their leaders.

The villages which were scattered over the country were connected by roads. In the central portion of the village were situated the quarters of the village headman, the chief's domains, and the meeting place of the village assembly.

For offensive weapons the Vedic Aryans have the bow and arrow, spear, dagger, and axe, and for defensive purpose they have the coat of mail.

The Vedic religion is aniconic. It reveals the struggle of the higher mind to get away from the concrete and to personify the aggregates of virtue in gods and goddesses. Although gods and goddesses are many and various, the Vedic religion envisages the conception of unity of the godhead. It keeps clear of the practice of Yoga but the Ṛgveda certainly contains some hymns that are definitely philosophical.

Section III

BRAHMANIC

During the period of the later Saṃhitās and the Brāhmaṇas, the growth in the complication of rituals led to the development of hierarchy of priests who began to assume an over-whelming importance in the estimation of people, for they were the guides through the wilderness of sacrificial arts. The Brahmanical priests have been raised to the position of gods. A Brāhmaṇa is regarded as the very embodiment of all duties. Mere birth in a Brahmanical family does not seem to have become the only title for the enjoyment of all the privileges to which a Brāhmaṇa is entitled. In return for his spiritual service a Brahmin is endowed with extraordinary rights and privileges. In no circumstances could a Brahmin be deprived of his property. The idea of priestly ascendency was carried to a pitch during the subsequent age of the *Sūtras* and the Epics. Side by side with the ascendency of the priestly class, we find in the Brāhmaṇa literature the tendency of other classes to harden themselves slowly into castes. The chariot-makers appear as a special caste along with the *Vaiśyas*. The importance assumed by the priestly caste during the Brāhmaṇa period could not eclipse the power and prestige of the princely class, for a *Kṣatriya* is regarded as the *Dharma* incarnate in the *Aitareya Brāhmaṇa*. The priestly class and the class of nobles or princely class were alike in advantageous position in the Vedic and immediately succeeding period, a position which the other two classes, viz., *Vaiśyas* and *Śūdras*, could seldom acquire. The Śūdras were more and more reduced to a subservient position. They were placed in the position of menials at the mercy of the upper three classes. The Śūdras though forming a part of society seem to have no social status in the Sūtra period. In the matter of marriage, the first and foremost question was the consideration of the clan or family to which the girl belonged. Consideration of caste could not always prevail in this matter. A person would ordinarily marry a member of his own caste. A Brahmin enjoyed the right of having a *Kṣatriya*, a *Vaiśya* or even a *Śūdra* girl as his wife. Women were gradually deprived of their former independence in the Brāhmaṇa period.

There was sugarcane plantation. The cultivation of hemp is mentioned in the *Atharvaveda* and *Śat*

Brāhmaṇa. People were mainly engaged in tilling the soil, keeping herds of cattle, tending their flock on pasture ground, and husking corns.

In the Brāhmaṇa period there were barbers, washermen, gatherers of wood, fishermen, herdsmen, huntsmen, professional musicians and acrobats, keepers of gambling houses, charioteers, door-keepers, cooks, butchers, wood-cutters, elephant-keepers, foot-soldiers, boatmen, manual labourers, astrologers, merchants, traders, messengers, waiters, bath-attendants and shampooers.

Among the persons practising arts and crafts during the Brāhmaṇa period mention may be made of the weavers, embroiderers, carpenters, chariot-makers, potters, black-smiths, workers in gold and jewellery, basket-makers, soap-makers, dyers, wine-distillers, actors, dress-makers, lute-players and courtesans. Women were engaged in some of the handicrafts, as for example, basket-making, dyeing, sewing, and embroidery.

The practice of medicine seems to have fallen from its original high standard and remained like a neglected calling.

In the Brāhmaṇa period we have the beginning of the metallic currency. There were gold coins, e.g., *niṣka, śatamāna.*

There were woollen and silk clothes and garments.

It was customary to entertain guests with meat of an ox or a goat. The sage Yājñavalkya is said to have been a beef-eater, a partaker of a type of meat of both milch cows and oxen.

The *Upaniṣads* with their literary background in the *Āraṇyakas* were the richest products of the early philosophical thought. They embody an *ātman* philosophy in the name of *Brahmavāda* or *Ātmavidyā* and contain the germs of all later Indian thoughts and religious ideas. The wide sweep of thought and imagination, all pointing to the conception of one single abiding reality, proceeds on a mystical insight into the depths of truth. The Yoga practice or *adhyātma yoga* cannot fail to indicate the continuity of the religious tradition of the Indus Valley civilisation.

Section IV

PRE-MAURYA

At the time of the Buddha and Mahāvīra, there were four classes of people or the four castes, viz. Khattiyas, Brāhmaṇas, Vessas and Suddas. The Khattiyas were superior to the Brāhmaṇas. Buddha did not lay much stress on the caste distinctions which, he said, were unscientific. The Brahmins were very proud of their caste. Besides, there were peoples of low castes, e.g., Caṇḍālas, Veṇas, Nesādas, Rathakāras and Pukkusas. The Caṇḍālas are distinguished from the Pukkusas, as corpse throwers from sweepers or methars. The Veṇas were workers in bamboo. The Rathakāras were workers in leather, and the Nisadas or Nesādas were the hunters.

In order to prevent the loss of colour through intermixture and to preserve the national, racial, tribal or family type, it was deemed necessary to impose certain restrictions as to *connubium* or the right of inter-marriage and *commensality* or the right of eating together. The re-marriage of women was not unknown. The birth of children particularly of male children determined the position of a married woman in her father-in-law's family and her happiness in married life. Prostitution was in vogue. Royal harem was filled with maidens and women of all grades.

The Purohita occupied a peculiar position in the royal household. The office of the Purohita was not necessarily hereditary.

There were the basket-makers, weavers, leather-workers, carpenters, metal workers, blacksmiths, goldsmiths, jewellers, potters, cloth-merchants, bow and arrow-makers, perfumers, tailors, dyers, fuel-suppliers, water-carriers, household servants, cooks, clerks, door-keepers, sentinels, drain-cleaners, sweepers, elephant-riders, elephant-trainers, chariot-drivers, foot-soldiers, wrestlers, bath-attendants, wagon-makers, money-exchangers, dyers, washermen, grass-cutters, sellers of sweetmeats, rice, fish, wine, etc., professional actors, acrobats, magicians, ballad-reciters, courtesans, dancing girls and slave girls.

Hereditary craftsmen, or those who followed professional callings, e.g., architects, mechanics, masons, butchers, and the rest, organised themselves into various guilds, agreeing to be governed by their own laws and customs.

The fields were cultivated by means of ploughs driven by oxen. Soil was turned with spades and watered by means of conduits. Various kinds of crops were grown on the soil. Rice was the chief article of food. Cattle were held in high esteem as a source of wealth. There were jungles all over the country. Trees were cut for wood and timber. Agricultural produces and industrial goods were sold in markets. There were inland land routes. A caravan consisted in some cases of 500 wagons and its course was guided by a land pilot. There were trade relations between Benares and Ujjain, Videha and Kāśmira-Gandhāra, Benares and Sāvatthī, Rājagaha and Sāvatthī, Magadha and Sauvīra. Foreign trade was carried on by sea. The commodities sold in shops were textile fabrics, groceries and oil, green groceries, grains, perfumes and flowers, etc. The hawkers carried their wares for sale in portable trays. The vice of adulteration was also not unknown.

Coins appear to have been the chief medium of exchange. Barter was not the usual practice. There were in use the letters of credit and promissory notes.

The early Buddhist texts refer to the four kinds of slaves and there were instances where the slaves were bought at a high price.

In Buddhism we find that the gods are broadly divided into three classes: (1) gods by common acceptance, (2) gods by origination, and (3) gods by purity. There were fire-gods, serpents, *yakkhas*, *asuras*, *Indra*, *Brahmā*, *Candra*, *Sūrya*, minor gods and quarter-gods. Hierarchy as developed in early Buddhism placed the four grades of *Arūpabrahmas* as the highest in the scale. The hierarchy as conceived in early Jainism seems to place the *Vemānikagods* as the highest in the scale. There were popular gods and goddesses affiliated to the realm of the four *lokapālas*. The Buddhist and Jain texts do not at all exaggerate the state of things when they inform us that secular Brahmanism consisted in spells, charms, incantations, exorcism, witchcraft, occultism, etc. In the 6th century B.C. people were believers in the efficacy of pronouncement of benediction by the priests and other holy persons, in amulets and the like. A vivid and fairly detailed picture of the life of the ancient order of hermits may be gathered. The tradition of hermit life was widely recognised as a well-ordered institution all over the Aryandom from Gandhāra to Videha and Kaliṅga and from Kuru-Pañcāla to Vidarbha.

The Jaṭilas used to wear matted hair on their head, garments made of birch-bark or antelope-skin. The Parivrājakas were the wanderers who were teachers or sophists spending 8 or 9 months every year wandering about precisely with the object of engaging themselves in conversational discussions on matters of ethics and philosophy, nature-lore, and mysticism. Like the Greek-sophists, they differed very much in intelligence, earnestness and honesty. There were leading thinkers and one of them was no other than Mahāvīra, the celebrated founder of Jainism. Some of the thinkers were wandering teachers, shavelings and mendicants and differed from the Parivrājakas as a class only in their attitude towards the world and the existing social and religious institutions. The Ājīvikas were the followers of Makkhali Gosāla, Nanda Vaccha and Kisa Saṃkicca. The Tāpasas, according to the Jaina *Aupapātikasūtra*, adopted the *vānaprastha* mode of life on the banks of the sacred rivers typified by the Ganges. They were either fire-worshippers, family men, or those who slept on the bare ground. They used the bark of a tree as their garment, and lived either on the sea-shore or near water at the foot of a tree, feeding on water, air, water-plants, roots, bulbs, barks, flowers, fruits and seeds.

The Buddha learnt the practice of *yoga* from the two great Yogis on his way from Rājagṛha to Uruvelā.

The early Buddhist mendicants belonged to a distinct religious order and school of thought, in respect of which the position of the Buddha was that of a Founder of an order, Leader of a following, and Teacher of a band of followers. The Buddha and his first disciples enthusiastically started the work of preaching the message under the fervour of a new-born faith. They stayed during the rainy season at the Deer Park during which the mendicants brought to the Master ardent applicants for initiation and ordination from various quarters and various localities. The great triumph was achieved when Sāriputta and Moggallāna were converted to the new faith together with the half of the other followers of the same famous teachers through the instrumentality of Aśvajit.

The admission of women into the Śākya Order was no novelty. Women enjoyed equal status with men. Among the Buddhist mendicants some figured as pioneers, some as preachers, chanters, learners, and the like.

Mahāvīra was a great teacher, a great guide, a great pilot, a great preacher, and a great recluse. He was a citizen of Vaiśālī (Modern Basarh in the Muzaffarpur District). He had a remarkable career as teacher for 30 years. He had an excellent community of 14,000 recluses with Indrabhūti at their head, 36,000 female recluses with Candanā at their head, 1,59,000 lay disciples with Śaṅkhaśataka at their head and 3,18,000 female lay disciples with Sulasā and Revatī at their head. He lived thirty years as a householder, more than twelve years in a state inferior to perfection, something less than thirty years as a Kevalin (the perfected one), forty-two years as a recluse, and seventy-two years on the whole. Those who came under the influence of his personality and teaching gave up the eating of meat and fish for good and strictly adhered to vegetarian diet. His great message to mankind is that birth is nothing, that caste is nothing and that *karma* is everything, on the destruction of *karma* the future happiness depends. Much importance has been given to soul, individuality and personality. The Jaina ethics has for its end the liberation or *mokṣa*. The three excellences are: right faith, right knowledge, and right conduct. The vows must be strictly observed by the monks. The *tapa* or austerity is divided into internal and external. Fasting is the most conspicuous form of austerity.

Both Buddha and Mahāvīra flourished at the same time. Buddha's life was well regulated and he assumed the position of a responsible preacher and reformer. He welcomed men of different faiths and discussed topics with them like a sincere friend. Self-exertion was the motto of his life and everywhere he laid stress on self-exertion, self-control, and self-sacrifice in his preachings. Sense of duty and responsibility was uppermost in his mind. He never lost his temper in hot discussions of the most difficult points of religion and philosophy with persons of different faiths. He never made a parade of his learning or achievement. He was never hostile to anybody, be he a friend or a foe. In his preachings and discussions there was a system throughout and the method followed was excellent. His life was a life of action, earnestness, wakefulness, simplicity, frankness, sincerity, perfection and order. He wandered from place to place and struggled hard to reach the final goal. In his wanderings he came into contact with the Parivrājakas, Śramaṇas and Brāhmaṇas, kings and peoples, and discussed with them various topics of religious, ethical, and philosophical importance. He gave up the path of self-mortification and sat down in meditation under the *Bodhi* tree till he attained the Supreme Knowledge.

In his First discourse, he laid stress on suffering, origin of suffering, cessation of suffering and the path leading to the destruction of suffering. The formulation of the four noble truths proceeded on the basis of the doctrine of Dependent origination, accounting for the origin and destruction of the entire mass of ill. He asked his followers to adopt the middle course which is called the golden mean in Buddhism. The noble eightfold path is undoubtedly the best method of attaining the internal purity of self which is nothing but *nirvāṇa*. *Nirvāṇa* means annihilation of passion, hatred and delusion. It is the waning out of all evils and the diminishing of the vicious and the weak in man. It is no doubt a blissful state of sanctification. In its negative aspect it means the going out of greed, ill-will, dullness, etc. and in its positive aspect it means mental enlightenment, conceived as light, insight, the state of feeling happiness, cool, calm and content, peace, safety and self-mastery. It really means truth, the highest good, a regulated life, communion with the best, etc. It is the tranquil state. It is secured from the worldly contact. It is the highest condition and the greatest happiness. The attributes of *Nirvāṇa* consist of absence of passion, destruction of pride, getting rid of thirst, freedom from attachment, and destruction of sensual pleasures and all sufferings.

The religion which Buddha preached spread far and wide and it has moulded the civilisation of countries and nations of the world. It is still followed by millions of people in all parts of the globe. His religion has really served to raise India in the estimation of the civilised world.

Education and learning were much advanced. *Itihāsa* was regarded in the Buddha's time as the fifth Veda; and according to the Jains *Nighaṇṭu* was considered as the sixth Veda. Kṣatravidyā or the science of archery or military science, and Tekicchā Śāstra or Āyurveda did not escape the attention of the early Buddhists. The science of music and the science of eugenics and erotic were much developed. The science of architecture too was known to the early Jains and Buddhists. Folk literature, astronomy, astrology, arithmetic, geography, rhetoric, and prosody were not neglected.

Takṣaśilā in the country of Gandhāra was an ancient seat of learning. The Brahmin youths, Kṣatriya princes and sons of bankers from Benares, Rājagṛha, Kośala and other places were either sent or went themselves for learning the various branches of arts and science. Besides there were other seats of learning e.g., Nālandā and Benares. In Buddha's time there were in Kośala and Aṅga-Magadha several *mahāsālās* or *snātaka* institutions maintained on royal fiefs granted by king Prasenajit of Kośala and king Bimbisāra of Magadha. There were also theological colleges granting admission only to the Brahmin youths.

SECTION V

MAURYA AND ŚUṄGA

Candragupta Maurya's imperial city, Pāṭaliputra, which was founded in the 5th century B.C., was defended by a massive timber palisade, pierced by sixty-four gates, adorned with 570 towers and protected externally by a broad and deep moat, filled by the water from the Son river. The royal palace chiefly constructed of timber was a magnificent one, its gilded pillars being decorated with golden vines and silver birds.

A wooden platform about 100 ft. long, 7 ft. high, and 5 ft. 6 in. wide, running north and south, was brought to light. The pedestals at Pāṭaliputra must have been of Persepolitan style. The Mauryan hall discovered at the site of the ancient city of Pāṭaliputra corresponds with the Persepolitan hall. The favourable site of ancient Pāṭaliputra made it a great centre of inland waterborne traffic.

The Superintendent of industrial arts was responsible for fixing the rates of wages. All foreigners were watched by officials who provided suitable lodgings, medical attendants, etc. Deceased strangers were decently buried and their estates were looked after. There was the systematic registration of births and deaths. Traffic in old goods either by sale or mortgage was prohibited unless sanctioned.

There were reporters whose duty it was to submit private reports with regard to all that was happening in the town or country. The rigour of criminal law was very severe.

The agricultural population was exempted from military service. There was a special irrigation department, charged with the duty of measuring the lands and regulating the sluices for allowing water to pass freely.

Strict control over all classes and castes of the population was exercised. The roads were maintained. There was a highly organised system of espionage. A regular system of excise licences was in force.

There was the town prefect (*nāgaraka*) who registered every arrival in or departure from his jurisdiction.

At the time of Candragupta's son Aśoka enormous sums were spent in the erection of the costly buildings in furtherance of his new faith. The Rock edicts of Aśoka give us a clear idea of his *Dharma*, which consists in docility to parents, liberality to friends, non-injury to living beings, self-mastery, purity of heart, gratitude, fidelity, toleration, compassion, truth and purity, etc.

The powerful bodies of preachers of Indo-Aryanism were able to create a cultural atmosphere throughout for the appreciation of different forms of the Indo-Aryan speech. The lofty message of *Dharma* lays stress on 'the dynamic of conduct'. Frequent meetings of the exponents of different faiths for a free discussion and interchange of thoughts and ideas were held to facilitate the scheme of toleration. Aśoka's efforts for the development of the national art and architecture of India proved fruitful. The four Rock-cut cave dwellings for the use of the Ājīvikas in the Barabar Hills, with a vaulted roof, an oblong, rectangular or circular outer chamber and bearing the distinctive characteristic of 'a bright polish shining from their walls as roofs' mark a glorious beginning of the cave architecture in India. The monolithic pillars similarly mark a proud beginning of the history of later Indian pillars of victory or ensigns of worship.

According to Aśoka there cannot be a nation without a true national feeling aroused and a national character formed. Similarly there cannot be nationality where the group of people belonging to it does not espouse a common cause of humanity, e.g., the elevation of human nature or the education of men to certain excellences of character. Aśoka openly declared that he had aspired in his heart of hearts to be a servant of the land, and that he had tried his level best to infuse this very idea into the mind of all his ministers, officers, and subjects.

The promulgation of the principle of the *Dharma* in the form of a humanised culture, was Aśoka's mission of life. It was a simple message of cultivation and development of life-forces inherent in human personality. Aśoka fully realised the true spirit of rationality and human greatness and he found it clearly set forth in the teachings of the Buddha. His dedication to a humanised culture was an indirect service to Buddhism. The Buddhist culture signified to him harmony and co-operation in human relationship. Through abiding peace among different peoples as a cardinal principle in the regulation of human affairs, the Buddhist culture could generate forces of social adjustment and understanding, co-operation and integration. In the realm of peace Aśoka saw the end of disintegrating and corrosive elements in the life of a nation. He expounded social philosophy of his own with a view to the promotion of the cause of piety and duty as among his subjects as among all men. As a real cultured man he approached 'the unconquered borderers' with a heart full of sympathy and affection. His officers and other agents were instructed in the spirit of his *Dharma* in order to achieve his ideal through them. Much stress should not be laid on the influence of the palace art tradition of Persepolis and Parsargadæ over the Asokan art and architecture. The former stands as an expression of pride and self complacence of the Achæmenians as victors and vanquishers of several nations, while the latter as an outstanding manifestation of the genuine human feeling for the eternal good of the world. Further we are beginning to see more and more clearly that the latter followed an art and cultural tradition which was India's own.

Under the Śuṅgas the Vedic rite of the horse sacrifice (*Aśvamedha*) was revived. A horse of a particular colour was consecrated by the performance of certain ceremonies and was let loose. The king or his representative followed the horse with an army and when the animal entered a foreign country, the ruler of that country was bound either to fight or to submit. If the liberator of the horse succeeded in obtaining the submission of all countries over which it passed, he returned in triumph, and if he failed, he was disgraced. After his successful return a great festival was held at which the horse was sacrificed.

The Śuṅga dynasty founded by Puṣyamitra made the first successful attempt to recognise the political and social ideas of Brahmanism. The popular form of Hinduism as presented in the Epics, the Hindu ideal of social and political life as taught in the Manusmriti, the revival of ancient vedic sacrifices such as the horse sacrifice (*Aśvamedha*), and the glorification of Sanskrit language as symbolised in the Mahābhāṣya of Patañjali are the chief features of revival of Brahmanical influence in the Śuṅga-Kāṇva period. The early official language predominantly *prakritic* was in a transitional stage and its growing tendency was towards Sanskrit. The outer railing of the Bharhut stūpa and the earlier railing enclosing the Bo-tree at Bodh-Gayā with their numerous sculptural decorations and ornamental gateways were definitely erections of this period. Similar erections at Sarnath may be relegated to this age. Some pillars were made in imitation of the monoliths of Aśoka but the available examples of the Śuṅga art go to show that already the tradition of high polish characterising the Asokan art was irretrievably lost. The sculptures at Bharhut exemplify a folk art utilised by the Buddhists for the glorification of their religion. The stereotyped heraldic devices which were undeniably derived from West Asian art appear to have no vital connection with the subject-matters of the Buddhist sculptures. There are no vestiges as yet of the Hellenic art tradition. The sun-god of Bharhut has nothing to do with the Greek representation of Apollo; it is typically the sun-god of Uttarāpatha. The oldest among the Bharhut figurines are masked and they remind us of the Egyptian art in some of their characteristics, particularly the frontal view, flatness, drapery, and lack of movement. But the art process did not remain stationary. From Bharhut to Bodh-Gayā it shows remarkable changes from sternness of monastic discipline to liveliness and vigour.

Section VI

SCYTHIAN

From Śuṅga-Kāṇva and Neo-Mitra age we pass into the pre-Gupta period during which Indian culture developed under the ægis of the Śaka-Kushāṇas, Śātakarṇis, Saharātas, Ikṣvākus and Kaikeyas. Here we find the north-western region of India, the very important centre of Græco-Buddhist art, particularly in Gandhāra.

In Kashmir numerous monuments were erected by Kaṇiṣka who founded a town there which still bears his honoured name. The celebrated Gandhāra sculptures found in large numbers in the Peshawar district and neighbouring regions bear ample testimony to considerable artistic merit to a modified Buddhism, a religion with a complicated mythology and well-filled pantheon. The flowery Corinthian capitals prove that the Gandhāra school was merely a branch of the cosmopolitan Græco-Roman art. The Gandhāra school reached its zenith of development in the 2nd century of the Christian era.

The great king Kaṇiṣka was a patron of learning. He had a poet like Aśvaghoṣa and a philosopher like Vasumitra in his court. His minister named Māṭhara, probably an exponent of the Sāṅkhya doctrine, was a man of unusual intelligence.

Under the patronage of Kaṇiṣka a Buddhist Council was held at Jullandar under the presidency of Vasumitra. Three extensive commentaries called *Vibhāṣas* were written. Hiuen Tsang says that the three Piṭakas with the commentaries were caused to be written on copper plates which were put in stone boxes deposited in a memorial mound. All these works survived in India and they now exist in Chinese translations or adaptations. Some of them have been discovered in original Sanskrit at Gilgit, particularly the whole of the *Vinayapiṭaka* of the *Sarvāstivāda* sect.

This age witnessed the development of the three different styles of Buddhist art and architecture, namely, the Gandhāra or Græco-Bactrian, the Mathurā or Indo-Ṣcythian, and the Amarāvatī or Indo-Roman. The Jaina art and architecture of Mathurā belong to the same Indo-Scythian style. A new cave-architecture developed in Northern India under the patronage of the Neo-Mitras and in Southern and Western India under the patronage of the Śātakarṇis. The Ikṣvākus and Kaikeyas were the patrons of the Buddhist art and learning in the Lower Kṛṣṇā Valley, at Amarāvatī, Jagayyapeta and Nāgārjunikoṇḍa. The division of the Jainas into two separate sects of the Śvetāmbaras and Digambaras, and the vigorous career of several Buddhist sects and schools of thought in both Northern and Southern India belong to this period. Here we are to notice the beginning of the Mahāyāna form of Buddhism along with the mystic cult of the Secret Society (Guhyasamāja). In the rock-cut caves caused to be made by the Jaina King Khāravela, his chief queen, son and officers, was laid the foundation of the Orissan art and architecture. Khāravela is known to have helped the people of Orissa in repairing the then existing Deva-temples as also to have built a grand Palace of Victory and a magnificent and costly religious edifice. While Prakrit continued to be inscriptional language in Southern and Eastern India, the official language was Sanskrit in the Middle Country and Western India. The first Sanskrit document of A.D. 150 is the Junāgaḍ rock inscription of Rudradāman I. This expressly bears testimony to the development of Indian poetics and dramaturgy. Aśvaghoṣa the poet paved the way for both Bhāsa and Kālidāsa through his kāvyas and Drama. The sūtras of the six systems of Hindu Philosophy, the production of the Bhagavad Gītā, the powerful dialectics of Nāgārjuna, and the Jaina treatise of Umāsvāti combine to speak of the richness and variety of the cultural development of this important transitional and formative age. Here one can trace the infant stage of Indian logic and theory of knowledge. Vātsāyana's *Kāmasūtra* (science of erotics) and Suśruta's great treatise on surgery speak eloquently of the advancement of scientific knowledge.

SECTION VII

GUPTA

The imperial Gupta period was chiefly a period of the development of Hindu culture and civilisation. Gupta coins and inscriptions refer to Vedic sacrifices which definitely point out that the Brahmanical religion considerably developed under the Guptas. The signs of *Garuḍa* and *Lakṣmī* on the official records indicate that the Guptas were ardent Vaiṣṇavas. It is evident from a Gupta inscription that the solar worship formed a prominent feature in the Hindu religion. Some of the Gupta inscriptions record grants of villages and lands to Brāhmaṇas. Donations are said to have been given for the maintenance of temples. The majority of inscriptions belonging to the Gupta period are Brahmanical in character. Sanskrit was adopted as the language of the inscriptions instead of Pali or other Prakrits. National life was very much influenced by Brahmanism. The Gupta sovereigns were remarkably tolerant towards other religions. The Gupta kings patronised two other contemporary religions, Buddhism and Jainism, in a variety of ways. It was with the permission of Samudragupta that his Ceylon contemporary, king Siri-Meghavaṇṇa, built a magnificent vihāra at Bodhgayā for the monks from Ceylon. The inscriptions of Kumāragupta II and Budhagupta refer to the images of Buddha set up at Sārnāth. Vasuvandhu and his brother Asaṅga developed Yogācāra philosophy along with the Vaibhāṣika system of Abhidharma. The earlier form of Mahāyāna called *Bodhisattvanaya* was properly systematised. During this period very few Jaina inscriptions are available. An inscription of Kumāragupta I records the setting up of an image of a Jaina Tīrthaṅkara at Mathurā.

As regards learning, the Mahābhārata reached its final shape and form. Sanskrit prose and poetry are seen to have been handled with great mastery. Hariṣena, Varāhamihira, Kālidāsa and Vāsula may be mentioned as ornaments of the Gupta period. The Gupta period is the Augustan age for the development of kāvyas and dramas, astronomy and astrology, philosophy and mathematics, logic and epistemology, architecture, sculpture and painting and various arts and crafts. The final redaction of the *Charaka-saṃhitā* was made in this age. Dinnāga founded the mediæval school of Indian logic and gave a systematic shape to the Indian theory of knowledge. Varāhamihira produced his masterly treatises on astronomy and astrology. Āryabhaṭṭa wrote his *Sūrya-siddhānta* and proved that the earth moves round the sun forestalling Galileo. Kumārılabhaṭṭa immensely developed the *Pūrvamīmāṃsā* into critical philosophy of orthodox Brahmanism. Vyāsa wrote his commentary on the Yoga system of Patañjali. The Jain Āgama was rehearsed for the last time at Valabhī and canonised. The Digambara Jainas came to have the *Ṣaṭkhaṇḍāgama* as their great book of authority. Buddhaghosa and Buddhadatta flourished as two great exponents of Pali Buddhism.

The corporation of guild-presidents, traders, and chiefs of groups of artisans was in existence. The Basarh seals give us ample information about the provincial and municipal administration as well as the economic organisation in the province of Tīrabhukti. During the rule of the Guptas the department of military finance was separated from that of civil finance. When a village was granted to any person or community, the villagers were required not only to render general obedience to the donees but also to pay them the usual dues from the village.

The grants of religious nature were usually perpetual, heritable, and exempt from several customary burdens of the village.

The weight of coins remained unchanged even during emergency.

SECTION VIII

LATER MEDIÆVAL

At the time of Harṣa, the famous Chinese pilgrim Hiuen Tsang visited India and saw several Buddhist monasteries. The most distinguished centre of learning was Nālandā which accommodated ten thousand students. Harṣa's gift to the university was a *vihāra* or a temple of brass or bronze about 100 ft. in height. The teachers and students at Nālandā were exponents or followers of different schools of thought and were always meeting in animated debates and discussions which so largely contributed to the development of the intellectual life of the University. The University claimed Śīlabhadra, Jñānacandra, Sthiramati, Guṇamati, Candrapāla, and Dharmapāla as the most distinguished scholars and teachers. Many secular and religious subjects were taught here. The hermitage of the Jain sage Divākaramitra was another seat of learning.

The most important popular deities of Brahmanical religion at the time were Viṣṇu, Śiva and Sūrya.

Harṣa forcibly secured from Kashmere the tooth-relic of the Buddha which he enshrined in a monastery built by him to the west of Kanauj.

Harṣa was noted for his pursuit and patronage of learning. He was endowed with poetical skill and originality and wide learning. Bāṇa, the author of Harṣacarita and Kādambarī, was the most distinguished of his literary proteges. Harṣa was a dramatist of no mean order. The dramas of *Ratnāvalī*, *Priyadarśikā* and *Nāgānanda*, are generally attributed to him. He wonderfully devoted himself to the task of depicting the emotions of self-sacrifice, charity, and magnanimity in his *Nāgānanda*.

At the time of Harṣa the cities were enclosed within quadrangular walls, broad and high. The walls were generally built of bricks but the walls of houses and enclosures were made up of bamboo or wood. The houses of the poor, thatched with common grass, were of brick or boards. Hiuen Tsang considers the architecture of the public buildings, Buddhist monasteries, to be most remarkable. Among the furniture there were corded benches, the frames of the seats were carved in different ways according to different tastes. There existed the idea of town-planning. Industrial life was organised on the basis of castes and corporations or guilds. The Brahmins had no part in the industrial life of the country. Trade and agriculture were in the hands of the Vaiśyas and Śūdras respectively.

There were various kinds of cloth then used, e.g., linen cloth, woollen cloth, inner clothing, outer attire, etc. Women used to wear long robes. Ornaments were freely used by the kings.

Society which was based on castes was governed by its rules. There were four castes forming four classes of various degrees of ceremonial purity. The Kṣatriyas and Brahmins according to Hiuen Tsang, were clean and unostentatious, pure, and simple.

There were bards, snake-doctors, goldsmiths, painters, musicians, pipers, shampooers, dancing girls, jugglers and scribes. There were also theatres, musical saloons and picture galleries.

Women of higher classes went in for education and did not live in complete seclusion. Admission into the royal harem does not seem to be very strict. The custom of *sati* or the voluntary self-immolation of widows on the funeral pyres of their husbands was then known. Queen Yaśovatī was the best example of a *Sati* described by Bāṇabhaṭṭa.

Sea-voyages were common. The facilities of shipping or navigation were called for by the needs of commercial and cultural intercourse between the countries. There was a brisk export of goods between India and countries beyond her borders.

In the early part of the 8th century A.D. a chieftain named Gopāla was elected king of Bengal. He was a pious Buddhist and founded a great monastery at Uddandapura or Otantapuri, a town of Bihar, which seems to have been at times the capital of the later Pāla kings. The famous monastery of Vikramaśila which is said to have included 107 temples and six colleges was founded by Dharmapāla. It stood on a hill overlooking the right bank of the Ganges. Devapāla, the most powerful of the Pālas, was zealous in the cause of Buddhism. Of all the Pāla kings, Mahīpāla I is best remembered, and the songs in his honour which used to be sung in many parts of Bengal until recent times, are still to be heard in the remote corners of Orissa and Cooch Behar. The great monastery at Nālandā was restored after it was burnt down by a man named Bālāditya who had emigrated from Kauśāmbī in the 11th year of Mahīpāladeva. His reign is marked by the re-establishment of Buddhism in Tibet. A mission headed by Atisa from the Vikramaśila monastery in Magadha during the reign of Nayapāla re-established Tibetan Buddhism. Several Buddhist *mahāvihāras* were founded in Bengal notably those at Somapura (Pāhāḍpur), Vajrayoginī (Vikramapur), Mahāsthān (Bogra) and Samataṭa (Tippera).

Buddhism although declining in India flourished in the Pāla dominions. The monasteries of Magadha were then crowded with thousands of residents. During the reigns of Dharmapāla and Devapāla, Dhīmān and Vītapāla, two artists of the time, acquired the highest fame for their skill as painters, sculptors and bronze-founders. During these reigns the Bengal sculpture reached its zenith. The sculptures of Magadha and Gauḍa became famous in India. Many Hindu and Buddhist stone images were carved. After the reign of Nārāyaṇapāla the sculpture of Bengal began to decline. No building of the Pāla age appears to have survived; but the numerous great tanks in the territories of the Pālas, especially in Dinajpur, testify to the interest taken by the kings in the execution of undertakings intended for the public benefit. All the Pāla kings were zealous Buddhists, ready to bestow liberal patronage on learned teachers and the numerous monastic communities. Devapāla appointed Sarvajñaśānti, a Buddhist teacher, as the head of the great monastery at Nālandā. Dharmapāla, a man of exceptional capacity, is credited with the merit of having been an ardent reformer of religion. His successors were devoted to Tantric forms of Buddhism and enjoyed the services of many pious men.

Ballālasena, a scion of the Sena dynasty founded by a chief named Samantadeva, was famous in the traditional history of Bengal. He is credited with having re-organised the caste-system and introduced the practice of Kulinism among Brahmans, Vaidyas and Kāyasthas. According to some he was the founder of Gauḍ or Lakhnauti. All the Sena kings were Brahmanical Hindus and therefore had a special reason for being hostile to the Buddhist Pālas. They had a keen interest in the maintenance of caste. The Hinduism of Ballālasena was of the Tantric kind. He is said to have sent numerous Brahmin missionaries to Magadha and other places. Buddhism as an organised religion in Bihar declined evidently due to the destruction of the monasteries which were the real strongholds of the Buddhist teachers. Lakṣmaṇasena, the ruler of Eastern Bengal, was endowed with the exceptional personal qualities. His reign was remarkable for considerable literary activity and for his liberal patronage of Sanskrit learning. An imitation of Kālidāsa's Meghadūta by Dhoyi, the court-poet of Lakṣmaṇasena, was published. Jayadeva, the famous author of the *Gīta-Govinda* seems to have lived in the reign of Lakṣmaṇasena who wrote verses himself. His father Ballālasena was also an author.

SECTION IX

ĀNDHRA AND DRAVIDIAN

The Āndhras in the days of Candragupta Maurya and Megasthenes were a Dravidian people and represented by a large population speaking the Telugu language. They occupied the deltas of the Godāvarī and Kṛṣṇā. The Āndhra country included 30 walled towns, numerous villages, and an army consisting of infantry, cavalry and elephants. The Āndhra kings claimed to belong to the Sātavāhana family and many of them assumed the title of Śātakarṇi. The Āndhra king Gautamiputra Śrī Śātakarṇi posed himself as the champion of the Brahmanical Hinduism and Buddhism as against the creed of casteless foreigners e.g., Śakas, Pahlavas and others. He gratified his Hindu sentiment by liberal donations to both Brahmins and Buddhists. It is interesting to note that although the Āndhra kings were officially Brahmanical Hindus, most of their recorded donations were made to Buddhist institutions. The Āndhras were an independent and civilised nation. The numerous and varied bronze and leaden coins of Yajñaśrī which formed the currency of the eastern provinces were in use. Some of these coins bear the figure of a ship which suggests the inference that Yajñaśrī's power was not confined to the land. Under them both Buddhism and Brahmanical Hinduism flourished. Almost all the Buddhist caves in the Deccan were excavated, villages and lands being granted to defray the cost of their maintenance, and to provide for the sustenance of the monks who inhabited the caves during the rainy season. The provision of new robes for these monks was secured by the investment of funds in one of the craft guilds. The Āndhra kings performed many sacrifices including the *Aśvamedha*, and *Gavāmayana* and paid heavy *dakṣiṇās* to the Brahmins. The worship of Śiva was popular and also the cult of Kṛṣṇa under the names of Saṃkarṣaṇa and Vāsudeva, while Indra and Dharma were widely revered. There seems to have been no antagonism between the two faiths, for the followers of Brahmanism excavated several caves for Buddhist monks, while the foreigners like the Śakas and Ābhīras freely embraced either religion and assumed Hindu names.

There were four classes of people at the time of the Āndhras in western India, the highest class being composed of the *Mahārathis*, the *Mahābhojas* and the *Mahāsenāpatis*.

The second class comprised both officials and non-officials. There were merchants, scribes, physicians, cultivators, goldsmiths, druggists, carpenters, gardeners, blacksmiths, fishermen, head of a trade guild, etc. The mercantile and cultivating classes were sub-divided into homesteads or families, the head of each was known as *gṛhapati* or *Kuṭumbin.*

The currency of the country consisted of kārṣāpanas which were both silver and copper, *Suvarṇas* or the gold coins and *Kuṣaṇas* or silver coins. There were many craft guilds, e.g., guilds of oil-pressers, hydraulic machine-artisans, potters, weavers, guilds of bamboo-workers, corn-dealers, etc. All these guilds acted as banks in which money could be deposited at interest. Permanent endowments such as those for religious purposes were publicly proclaimed and registered in the records of the town-assembly.

There was a flourishing foreign trade in western India. Ships from the west sailed down the Red Sea to Broach and the Malabar coast, which supplied the two great inland marts of Paithan and Tagara and possibly visited the two harbours of Sopārā and Kalyān.

The Coḷa country was drained by the river Kāverī and comprised the districts of Trichinopoly and Tanjore. *Coḷa-maṇḍalaṃ* or the Coḷa-country stretched along the eastern coast from the river Pennar to the river Vellar and on the west reaching to about the borders of Coorg. Tamil is as much the vernacular of the Coḷas as of the Pāṇḍyas and no clear ethnical distinction can be drawn between the peoples residing north and south of the Vellāru which is the southern limit of the traditional Coḷa country. The kingdom of the Coḷas which was unknown to Pāṇini, was familiar to Kātyāyana and recognised by Aśoka as independent. The ports on the Coromandel or the Coḷa coast enjoyed the benefit of active commerce with east and west. The Coḷa fleets boldly crossed the Bay of Bengal to the mouths of the Ganges and Irrawaddy as well as the Indian ocean to the islands of the Malaya archipelago. All kinds of goods imported into Kerala or Malabar from Egypt found a ready market in the Coḷa country. The western ports drew a large part of their supplies of merchandise from the markets of the eastern coast which produced great quantities of cotton goods. The principal Coḷa port was Kāviripaddinam. It was once a wealthy city containing a magnificent palace of the king. The Coḷa kings were alleged to belong to the tribe of Tiraiyar or men of the sea. The Coḷas were a very ancient people, as we find them mentioned in the Rock Edicts II and XIII of Aśoka.

The Pāṇḍya kingdom comprised the greater part of the modern Madura and Tinnevelly districts and also southern Travancore. It was famous for skilled craftsmen, and families of eighteen guilds lived there. There existed a close cultural relationship and constant intercourse between south India and Ceylon, the notable centres of Buddhist learning being Kāveripaṭṭana, Madurā and Kāñchipura.

Early Tamil poetical literature supplies us with an interesting information of the ancient state of society. The Tamils had developed an advanced civilisation of their own. The prevailing religion was demon-worship. The immigrants from the north who settled at Madura and other cities tried to introduce Hindu notions of castes and ceremonials. The aboriginal devil worship exposed to the persistent attacks of Jainism, Buddhism and Hinduism, was gradually forced into the background. In the Pāṇḍya country the decline of Jainism began in the 7th century A.D., but the religion continued to flourish in Mysore and the Deccan for some ages after that time. Slavery was unknown among the ancient Tamils. The Tamil land had the good fortune to possess three precious commodities, viz., pepper, pearl, and beryl. The pearl fishery of the southern sea attracted a crowd of foreign merchants. The pepper fetched an enormous price in European markets. The beryl was greatly esteemed both by the Indians and the Romans. The Tamil states maintained powerful navies.

The Augustan age of Tamil literature may be placed in the first three centuries of the Christian era. Poetry, music, drama, painting and sculpture were cultivated with success. The plays are said to have been of two kinds; *the Tamil* or indigenous and *Aryan* or northern.

The Pallavas are believed to have risen to prominence before the middle of the 4th century A.D. The Pallava kings performed Aśvamedha sacrifices.

The fine examples of Pallava architecture are to be found at Conjeevaram, Mahabalipuram, Trichinopoly, Tanjore and Pudakottai. The Pallava architecture may be divided into two groups: the rockcut and structural. The remarkable feature of this architecture is the high quality of the figure sculpture which adorns both the *maṇḍapas* (pavilions) and *rathas* or monolithic temples.

The Chālukyas claimed to be a race of Rajputs from the north, who imposed their rule upon the Dravidian inhabitants of the Deccan tableland. Pulakesin I, a Chālukya king, is said to have asserted his claim to a paramount position by celebrating an Aśvamedha. During the time of the Chālukyas a large fresco painting in cave I at Ajantā is of the highest value as a landmark in the history of pictorial art.

During the two centuries of the rule of the early Chālukya dynasty of Vātāpi, Buddhism, although still influential, was slowly declining and suffering gradual supersession by its competitors, Jainism and Brahmanical Hinduism. The Pauranic forms of Hinduism grew in popularity. Everywhere elaborate temples dedicated to Viṣṇu, Śiva or other members of Pauranic pantheon were erected. The orthodox Hindus borrowed from their Buddhist and Jain rivals the practice of excavating cave temples; one of the earliest temples of this kind is that made at Badami in honour of Viṣṇu. Jainism was specially popular in the southern Maratha country. The religion of Zoroaster was introduced into India during the 8th century A.D. The reign of Krishṇa I, a Rāṣṭrakūṭa king, is memorable for the execution of the most marvellous architectural freak in India. The Kailāsa monolithic temple at Ellora is the most extensive and sumptuous of the rock-cut shrines.

Under the Rāṣṭrakūṭas much bitterness was introduced into the wars of this period by the hostility between the rival religions, Jainism and orthodox Hinduism. Under them Sanskrit literature of the artificial type was liberally encouraged. Vikramāṅka considered his achievement sufficiently notable to justify him in establishing a new era running from A.D. 1076, called after his name. Vijñāneśvara, the author of Mitākṣarā, the chief authority of Hindu Law outside Bengal, and the celebrated jurist of his time, used to live in the capital city of Vikramāṅka.

In A.D. 1167 Southern India was marked by a religious revolution effected by a revival of the cult of Śiva and the foundation of a new sect called the Liṅgāyat. The members of the Liṅgāyat sect were numerous in the Kanarese districts. They worshipped Śiva in his phallic form, rejected the authority of the Vedas, disbelieved in the doctrine of re-birth, objected to child marriage, approved of the re-marriage of widows and cherished an intense aversion to Brahmins. The growth of this new sect which secured many adherents among the trading classes checked the progress of Buddhism and Jainism.

During the twelfth and thirteenth centuries Hoysala chiefs attained considerable power in Mysore. During the early years of the reign of the first notable Hoysala prince named Bittideva, Jain religion enjoyed high favour under the protection of his minister and the damaged Jain temples were restored. The king was converted to Vaiṣṇavism under the influence of the celebrated reformer Rāmānuja who received his education at Kāñci. The well-known philosopher lived at Śrīraṅgam during the reign of Adhirājendra. He had to leave it owing to the hostility of the king who was a Śaiva. After his death, Rāmānuja came back to Śrīraṅgam where he resided till his death. The magnificent buildings at Belur and Halebid amply testify to his zeal and good taste. He assumed the name of Viṣṇuvardhana or Viṣṇu.

During the reign of the Yādava king Rāmachandra, the celebrated Sanskrit writer Hemādri popularly known as Hemādpant flourished. He devoted himself mainly to the systematic redaction of Hindu religious practices and observances and compiled important works on Hindu Sacred Law.

From the 2nd or 3rd century A.D. onwards the intellectual centres were shifted to south India. The Buddhist monasteries at Amarāvatī, Jageyyapeta, and Nāgārjunikoṇḍa in the lower Kriṣṇā valley became the meeting places of all the earlier Buddhist sects. Nāgārjuna, the powerful Buddhist dialectician, Buddhadatta, Buddhaghosa and Dharmapāla, the three notable Buddhist commentators, Kumārilabhaṭṭa, the famous exponent of *Pūrvamīmāṃsā*, Śaṅkarācārya, the founder of Advaita School of Vedānta, and Kālakācārya, the distinguished Jain teacher, were all the great celebrities of south India and best representatives of Indian thought.

INDEX